ATOM CITY

poems by

Sara Sams

Finishing Line Press
Georgetown, Kentucky

ATOM CITY

ACKNOWLEDGMENTS

"Scene with Granny and Lightning" and "Prophecy After the Death of a
Daughter" first appeared in *Chapter House Journal*.

"Appraisal Report: Atom City" first appeared in *Now & Then: The
Appalachian Magazine*.

"Medical" first appeared in *Volta* Issue 45.

"Deploying" first appeared in *Matter Monthly*.

"Maricopa County Blues" first appeared in *Four Chambers Press*.

"Decayed Ghazal" first appeared in *Spectral Lines*, an anthology published by
Alternating Currents Press.

Publisher: Leah Huete de Maines
Editor: Christen Kincaid
Cover Art: Kristin Apple
Author Photo: Bojan Louis
Cover Design: Elizabeth Maines McCleavy

Order online: www.finishinglinepress.com
also available on amazon.com

Author inquiries and mail orders:
Finishing Line Press
P. O. Box 1626
Georgetown, Kentucky 40324
U. S. A.

Table of Contents

For Billy Paul, who taught me how to shape questions,
and for Billie Dólii, who has since taken up the charge

I. ATOMS OF THE BODY

In the vast archive of an infinitely divisible space and time, you are an atom: single and indivisible: a *hypothetical body*."

—Akira Mizuta Lippit, Atomic Light (*Shadow Optics*)

BUT THINK, ARE YOU AUTHORIZED TO TELL IT

I didn't know the secret
we kept when I lived in the town
where quiet vines thread trees in winter.
Now I visit every year
to see the trumpet creeper
gone brown and the kudzu
like dead party streamers,
and today there was a squirrel
eyeing me from his side,
the way a squirrel
must. He clattered
on the roof and
called for me
to speak more plainly,
so I'll shoot for pared-down.
A small phrase
to hold and turn over,
a coin with two sides—
cool and smooth
and seductive, like security.

You could bite the coin
to test the secret;
or lay it on an eye
as you sleep, just for
the quality of the image.
Electrons dance inside metal
like dreams.

Walking deep
through greenway trail,
I listen to the story
of Tsutomu, who made it home
from Nagasaki to Hiroshima
after one white flare
in time to see the second.
Then I sit on a root

shiny with sap
from a higher wound,
tooth down on what
I'm meant to share with you.
The hard coin whirs
against my tongue:
I don't believe I've ever been quiet
just because I was told.

PROPHECY AFTER HEARTBREAK

John Hendrix, "local prophet"
Oak Ridge Valley, Tennessee, 1902

She left me and I missed being touched—
that's the reason I went barefoot
through the woods. Bare feet
give one the sense

of being intimate. The dirt tickled me;
          a speck of oak lodged
between my toes. Then I saw two streams
          run out in opposite directions,

though they laid beside each other.
          This struck me, called to me
like my long-gone wife. *Listen here,* the streams said:
          Listen better.

If I say *God, how the earth of her would shake*—
          you figure I'm prone to exaggerate.
But you're imagining our love, now,
          which is good. It's what people

forget. You can call love *God* if you like. I lay down
          because I missed her and because desire
is a kind of god, we all know that.
                    When the ground kept whispering

I pressed an ear down.
          Of course I called it god; by now you know
that men around these parts will do that:
          hear a woman's breath from deep within,
say it's godlike.

                    Which is the point: *listen better.*
                    I listened so long
I got hungry, like when we used to lie all day in bed.

In that state I dreamed,

        listening, listening. I could hear
what was brewing here, as if the seed of disease—
    the sound both strange and close to home,
as my belly rumbles in a fight.

    And in the rumbling
I heard, yes, the pounding down of railroad ties,
     and yes, the rushed-up factories for the bomb.
     (I think I had the word for bomb.)

How they'd enlist
    all this I've said
as platform for their story,
     all "Here John saw the atom split!"

      and "Here John spoke God's plan!"
But I was trying to say
    I hear you.   I was trying to say
Come back home, now.

APPRAISAL REPORT: ATOM CITY

What it's worth depends on who you ask. What it's worth depends on who asks. Do you take into account the dogwoods, the squid-ink blue of storm formed just behind the ridge; do you take into account the mud slung to raise temporary housing, the enemy dead, the length of lines for cigarettes, and so forth. How do you calculate such patient waiting and other acts of patriotism. Do you file the picture of the schoolgirl, 1995, hair-on-end, smiling for the camera? But then what do you do with the photo once it's been filed? Do you refer to it here, in this report? You might. But then you'd have to refer to the lot of them—and there's a whole lot more; this is an entire city, after all, containing multitudes of molecules and wise-cracked smiles. The city's pride sits in the center of town, adjacent to the derelict hotel, standing like a Shining on the hill. Start there: It measures 20 x 10 x 20—quite large in scale if you consider the unit of measurement, but is it stable, will it hold? Ask the right questions. If you want to know its real worth, you'll have to look out back. Is there a privy? If so, no indoor plumbing at all, and that's a problem. Big enough and standing, that's one thing, but sooner or later someone's going to have to take a shit. How will you assess all that sewage piling up? What is the standard of value of a smell? Is it balanced by the charcoal drift, the damp green scent pressed on you by the fog? What about the pungent urine samples in small, unlabeled vials? Other items are less discrete, but nonetheless important: How about *location*, do you rate the mountain views, the distance from Japan? Do you take into account the Friendship Bell? Stand inside the dome while the clapper swings. How's your head. Are any of these conditions actually better than "fair"?

PROPHECY AFTER THE DEATH OF A DAUGHTER

First spiraled mint and knock-kneed peddlers,
then her small face, bright as a city not yet built.

Then the candy resting on her tongue
like a stone, the *rud rud* of a wagon wheel,

a particle of dust in my eye. Then three fathers'
worth of trinkets, their future value resting not

on material or use but on their distance past
so many rolling hills of time, so long

before the great unsettling. But first,
her skin stretched like a too-still pond.

Now my foot on a puddle, pushing down.
Now a burial and a hinge and me falling off.

A wife unwilling to distract herself with God,
the voice coming from beneath the puddle.

Now the wife gone. Next, a long time on the same ground
that took my neon girl; the echo of a word

I know but never learned. Then white fungus
growing too fast beside me, as if sprouting from

my cheek. Soon, the pure white of a star and a pain
in my temple. Soon, a collective upturning

of bellies. Soon, a new museum
and, beneath the stairs, a photo of

a shadow of a boy—right where
the boy had been. Soon

a woman with pond-colored eyes
will visit, say *it had to be.*
Does that make this a prophecy?

THINK OF SLEEP

Of lungfuls sweet as licorice,
of air that lazes in
and out of houses.

Of a needle pushed
between the sun-burst
triangles on a quilt.

Are you there, yet?
It's a two-room
and childless cabin,

built on John the Prophet's
second lot, his first lot
flooded by the dam.

A woodstove, characteristic
of that time, sits
but doesn't burn

in the center of a dark room.
Think of the night
that surrounds you,

and of John, because he's out
there in it. Look deeper,
at the purplest;

think of your own
passions. Of the metal
whir when canned goods open.

Of how your nostrils flare
at this tart and illusory
blueberry jam—

is the *blueberry* you smell
prescient, or just
the kind of jam

your grandmother made
in her old house—
her house that's gone, now, too?

You think about staying here
with him, in his cabin,
or worse, leaving him there

as your mind moves like water
onto and over other things.
A thin rattle shakes below you,

a brown paper sack
rubbing against itself, the sound
of your grandmother,

scooping through her lowest
cabinets for a pan. Don't worry,
you think, *don't worry,*

you say out loud
in the restlessness
you find yourself in,

after your husband drifts
so quickly off to sleep:
Think of how John woke

from his long illness, after
many months alone. Remember he
remarried. You are the intruder,

here, in John's old story:
Falling down the night's dark spine,
you can easily forget

about a bomb
that never touched
you. What you do instead

is start to count the days
it was until John's second
wife appeared;

you use your fingers,
press them down, *one-
two-three-four-five,*

one-two-three-four-five, again
and again into the skin-soft
threading of your sheets.

Is it a surprise, by now,
how you've soaked history
through and through

with your desires? —
remembering the ghost
that cradled you,

once, so sweetly
and with such longing,
as you slept?

THE GENERAL

If God up above wants you so dumb
What kinda devil does that make him?
　　　　—King Dude, Valley Bar, Phoenix 2015

My body is loose with a bad
Tennessee whiskey

and B., Moody & I
are all all lulling

our heads to a song that,
along with the whiskey,

makes my grandmother
pray for us from her grave.

I'm thinking of my first love,
how he'd cup my body

on my star-felt sheets
and tell me all he wanted

to do was sleep.
When he left me

for a military academy,
I threw a lamp across

the room to scare myself
back into the body he'd loved.

"He's probably a general now,"
I slur, learn he trains people

how to kill people for a living,
because Moody googles him
right there at the bar,

11

has me spell the name
correctly till I repeat the letter k

like a mantra, feel a fiber jolt
through me that I'd like to

tell you was an echo of love,
but was really a grief all for me,

an ache for that girl
standing in her room,

holding her arm out for
the light she's just thrown.

HOME SALON

Aunt Margaret enjoys the springing action of the curl,
        the little bundle of her mother's being—
how it coils around itself as if the present were absurd,
        reaches back toward an earlier time when

these roles were reversed. It's not that she becomes
        or is becoming her mother but that another line is blurred,
the one that says everything is immediately true or has passed,
        that Margaret is either or, a line for practical purposes.

This is why when her mother dies she *tsks* the mortician,
        the prim contours he shapes with her hair, how he obscures
the energy they'd contained in the windings they'd made
        of each other for half a century; why her scalp

is still pricked and pricked by the other's fingers
        spidering through her; why Margaret takes the plastic cylinders
from her pocketbook and grips their sea-foam-colored curves.
        This won't do, she is saying, this won't do.

GRAPEFRUIT TREE

for Naira, 1988-2017

We want to use the word *bloom.*
Even a pitcher plant, phallic in glory,
blooms. We want to see the petals
pushing out, and since we have no deal
with time, we stupidly unfurl our mouths.
Nouns that have been said to:
onion, algae, mushroom cloud;
daughter, cancer. This last because
we like to trick ourselves
into a vast perspective,
one that slides more easily into
absence. Today the trick has failed me.
What does it say about us that,
even knowing what we know of matter,
we still see ourselves as whole,
steady? At five sweet pollen
glides into my room.
How beautiful the word, *citrus.*
How eager I am to write it down.

THIS BIT HERE COULD GO

You'd see my restlessness if you were to catch me, leering at myself in the bathroom. Not like she who tucked her thigh into a canister of tights, plastered her waist, and shaped herself into a handle. There's no sexual pout staring back at me as I look for the dimple's dimple, the twitching glute. I think I might be entering a dissociative state, and I have to say, it's fucking thrilling. When I struggle to find the words to explain, Rachel helps me, gives me *ambivalent*, and she's right. This bit here could go. Whatever. Maybe because lipids kept my father's heart from reaching the potential of its emblem, a symbology that's held me through three decades of small and large despairs. I was in Lyon when the slow descent inside him started without notice—was there a parade of color, there? Merlot to cherry to blush to salmon, greyed at the edge? Did it happen as I found my way to stadium seats, eager to watch the game? I would like to google congestive heart failure now, to try and faint. That'd knock me out of my reverie, wouldn't it? Instead I bulge up and pull at myself, making me think of the baguette I'd been eating, roasted chicken with a piquant honey mustard; what warmth it brought to my belly, how badly I needed that warmth just then, for the stadium mouth opened up to an endless fog, *un ciel de fumée d'argent*, and I had walked a long way and missed my father. I remember the sky that night exactly as I found it in a French poem, one year later, after he was gone.

APPRAISAL REPORT: SINGLE ATOM IN AN ION TRAP

after the photo by David Nadlinger

emitting just the right blue-violet light
        not this blue   not this violet
        not this blue   not this violet
blue and violet like irradiated want
        like *Taco Bell*   like fat and acid
sliding down my throat

I catch on *motionless*
        on what I *bulge up and pull*
        everything the sea is not
motionless pricks
motionless is rigid clamp
is out of time

I buoy my worry
like a cross-stitch
set against velour

cross-stitch blue
as the houses
of my hormones
        peptide honeycombs
        pristine chambers
        complicated trash
        put out back

speck better than the purple
squish consolidating
at the nave of the toilet

speck of endless voraciousness
        to maketo have

speck that urges me to say *multitudinous*
the word in my mouth
nearly motionless
nearly seen

speck almost what I want it
to be   the image from
a song we once sang
        Particle Man
        Particle Man

the idea of scope spreading
in my nine-year-old brain
        like mold
        like rot on a banana

SCENE WITH GRANNY AND LIGHTNING

1930

There's a cold pail by my feet
        when lightning's shucked
from roof to cow to thumb—
        makes me buzz
near how licking hail does:

Now me, all quiet-like,
        and the door stuck
just as pitiful to the barn,
        which course starts up shaking.
What a rapturous priss of a storm

we're in, her grand finale
        as frantic as a whooping
cough, akin to engine failure,
        —how when I dance
my limbs'll tremble as they loosen,

then wilden, then let
        a small bundle of intimates out
to who knows where.
        Cows don't like this. A cow
likes routine. So I make biscuits,

though what milk I have
        is scorched.
It's three months from here
        my sister goes, too young
to know it. When they lower

her—sound like a cast iron
        slung to the back of the rack—
the selfsame tremor
        finds me. My body
hums

out after her,

through the hinge

II. ATOMS FROM YOUR HOMETOWN

"The name change symbolized [General Leslie] Groves's larger program of duplicity: to hide the project in plain sight, to recast necessary but unsavory violations of law, logic, and custom by setting them within a new language-environment."

—Peter Bacon Hales, *Atomic Spaces*

ED WESCOTT DEVELOPS AERIAL UNDER GOVERNMENT SUPERVISION

photo of Hiroshima from National Archives

Your first view of me:
a single streetcar

and a wave of sticks.
Adjust the iris:

now I'm an array
of grey-black discs.

Why would they be guarding this?
Do you remember

your grandmother's grin?
Breathe her onto me;

she should last until I clear
to wreckage. My assembler,

with your acid wash and developing tank,
how did my knock-kneed poles

survive your light?
What a little boy you

once were, how much you loved
her dumplings, how she would sculpt them

by hand. Neurons fire up
a chain-reaction, too. Suck in air and

spit it out, do what you
always do to get the shot.

Why do you think they want me?
What of my three bicycles,

my men left standing?
Ride the strip

down the middle of me, a cleaner
blank. Where do I take you?

Where will I take them?
Will you ever let me

take you there again?

MANTELPIECE

There's a missing picture you might call
June the year Dad died—
the Warriors and the Cavaliers,
mosquitos and cigarettes,
other smells and sounds. But now
when I make my way toward it,
through the backyard thick with undergrowth,
through honeysuckle and poison ivy
and toward the tall itchy grass of open lawn;
when I head up the backstairs
and compel myself over the porch
his bed once faced
and open the kitchen door, the one next
to the bin that always needed
emptying—when I finally inch by
his living room chair,
there's nothing to find
but a thin rectangle of dust
on a thicker layer of dust.
What the frame left behind.

WHAT YOU SEE HERE

—Jackson Square, 1942

The family physicist is in the store
       with his wife.
A visible heat

augments his cheeks
       next to
three shins stretched

in nylon seams.
       He turns away
from the unreal feet, knowing

his wife's panties
       are where they should be.
Then he sees two silk bows

       flashing like a back-blast
in his periphery. If you see this,
       then you don't see: The slot

in the department wall
       like a lost gap inside her,
into which, when he goes,

she will drop her love for him;
       A letter licked shut
and hers the tongue that wet it.

You don't see whose hands
       thumb through
the pool of immaculate,

school-grown code,
       each loop curling
like lips around a secret.

Instead you see
        what the physicist sees
after leaving her

and all that hosiery:

A pyramid of pert green bottles,
        a snap-top lid,
and his own two nostrils

standing at attention.
        You, too, smell the new shampoo.
It's clean but synthetic,

like the film that wraps
        each day he spends inside the lab
without her. You come to know

        how the sunset always shocks him
when he leaves,
        how he'll see the rays

through a puff of cloud
        and think of her fingers
working a roller out.

        And now you have the vivid
if inaccurate sight he's had
        but once or twice

of the sun setting in the opposite
        direction, of darkness spreading up
                from the horizon.

        Does your head now hurt
the way only five o'clock
        sun can hurt you?

Then you know,
        as he knows, that the image
of her hair won't fade

from the evening sky.
        Instead, he sees each blonde wave
turn black and even the box

she bought, emptied
        of its dye on the counter.
In his daydream, it's her point

        to scare him and to let him know
she scares him because she loves him,
        equally: *My husband, The Physicist,*

she says as the black spills out
        from the pressure of his own hands
on his temples. *My husband,* she says

until her face goes gaunt and gaunter,
        until it's lucky that the billboard cuts
against the western sky,

makes a geometry of his wrong-seeing.

PERHAPS "LUCKY" IS TOO CASUAL

This Christmas, they've dug up
the stadium grass so deep
I can smell vanilla lip gloss

from the hill; I can see
my seventeen. She's in low-rise
jeans and a sports bra,

her belly painted for the game.
Her face opens up *belonging*
as if it were an orb

she might extend
to all her crushes, even the girls
who'd like to ruin her—

at least for the duration of the game—
all of them under the atom sign,
cheering for their team.

The chant is vile,
the other team getting screwed
or them screwing us,

maybe, and then there's John,
the local prophet,
his head a great solar eclipse

on my memory,
blotting out Blankenship Field.
He's comical in the hat

he wore while busting out of

country farm; he sighs
and sucks in fog through

gritted teeth. I think to ask
about his vision,
the one that made him myth,

but the plow's back
at it, now, so I rush
to what I want to know,

why I got to grow up happy
in a town that knitted
mushroom clouds.

When he speaks
again, the sound is cold
and picks me clean:

STOCKPILING WITH LEÓ SLIZÁRD

Let us collect what would keep us here,
dear Leó, circling and circling

the selfsame valley, trying to look
directly at what could pull us in.

Let us set aside the sludge of our guilt:
the scabs at your cuticles, scrubbed

too-clean; magnolia leaves that would
clog the basement drain, cause a flood;

the ghost of a woman recently passed,
whose house I lease for the summer—

who seems to be and not to be here,
a simultaneity that stares me dead

in the eye each night. Let us wring
the sweat from the clothes of ourselves,

drop each bead into a drum.
Set aside, science man, everything

that compels you to scoff: This world,
in all its curious hairiness, is no longer

yours to plait and de-plait
at will. This is for show.

Fill one drum entirely with your nightmares,
and I will do the same—in one

over here, dead man, my dog is nearly
drowning and I cannot save her,

cannot keep her head up high enough,
though I try desperately, scream and kick

my partner in his sleep. This particular slush,
you should know, from naming my dog

after a man killed in a distant war,
a war that reaches me here in a mist

of abstractions. Not just Lorca's war:
All wars reach me by abstraction.

We fill another drum entirely
with misremembered paragraphs,

texts that meant to make me question,
then forget, my guilt. We set aside

this tendency of ours to question;
we collect what we must to leave

it all drummed away, here,
waiting for disposal.

MEDICAL

Run two fingers over your nipple
as instructed by the pamphlet: *a smooth,
circular motion*, how a jar sings.

                 —The squirrels
that burrowed
in your bedroom walls
to scratch a home out   —Buds
relentless inside a body

                 —The man-made pond
you used to skim for fish,
a vibrant green and pedestrian bridge.

Progress toward the perimeter:
Your fingers should make tiny laps
the size of quarters, as if your own small moon.

                 —A rush of rainbow scales
like streaks of blush
                 —A hundred down-turned faces
of trout
                 —Your little dimpled
self in the tension of a line

RESEARCH

When you remember the Museum
of Science and Energy, you remember

your mom's way of patting rouge on her lips
so gently, it's as if she's pressing a pie crust.

She was eager to help with your research,
affirmed the bomb was a terrible

and sad and necessary thing. Consider
the use of calling a bomb *thing*.

Consider: Is it best to hear this from she
who breast-fed you? Remember

the photography exhibit, its walls carpeted
in *kiss-me red* but still missable,

tucked behind the gallery stairs
like an errant hair. Look at yourself:

So intent on looking you began to feel
yourself worth seeing. You remember

tidying your hair, wild from
humidity, then reading the simplistic

captions, flitting back between
the photo of the shadows and the

Ladder, Boy
the Ladder, Boy

Where
Had Been.

Even now, you see your mom's lips loosen—
helium falling, a line gone slack. Remove

your palm from the generator, that metal sphere
you volunteered, on a fourth-grade trip, to touch;

feel your fibers loosen, too—then fall,
after standing years, involuntarily, on end.

MANUFACTURING

You can't remember his joke but you know
        it had to do with squirrels. You're
trying to coax the story out:
        Afternoon sun squeezed through trees,
leaves that pirouette across the carpet's
        pale-blue seams, and Anna's dad,
a safety engineer, rocking slowly, a show of effort
        at his weakest. Maybe they weren't squirrels,

but atoms. Might be, as the chair runners edge back
        like two warped smiles
 "Two atoms walk into a bar" he says,
        winking at Anna. "And it's apparent
one of these atoms is in trouble,
        cause he's wearing this cheeseball grin—
you know, the one you give me
        when you can't find your keys?"

"Yeah," she says, "I know the look,"
        the look that brings me
back here, to his house, the look
        that wants to scour him of the rot
he'd volunteered to take. "Anyways,"
        I remember now, "Anyways," he says,
"this atom says to the other
        atom, *Shucks, I've lost an electron,*
and his friend, seeing the dilemma, asks:
        Are you sure?
                Yes, the atom replies, *Yes. I'm positive.*"

DEPLOYING

Every use becomes a metaphor

    for using. Every metaphor for using

becomes a reason for using, a link in the chain

    that has evolved into a chain of pure thought,

a chain that fattens or shrinks as a thought

    may fatten or shrink in any given moment, untouched

as it goes in the grove of the mind. Each tree

    makes way for the next while managing

to feed itself fully on the light. Wait.

    Were we speaking of metal or

of wood? Am I lost?

    The goal, after all:

The word Manhattan

    is a woman wishing so much

for affection

    that no one will give her any;

and, for added irony,

    the general's home address. Reorient.

As he would say, *Recast necessary but unsavory*

violations of logic, not

see what is possible, but

see what is possible

through.

Seen through, his *language-environments*

have grown greedy, speak

nuclear heritage,

define bomb

as *birthright.* Ask:

Was your grandfather in the war?

Does your dad work at the lab?

Why are you writing about this, again?

TARGETING

We have been assaulted by green, our eyes so washed through
      with green that any other shade—

a mistake of brown, a leaf knocked down by sudden rain—
      makes in us a desire to clean.

So saturated, on a porch hugged tight by
      humidity, magnolia, poplar and bush,

the static bumble of globed bees,
      I think of a word I've learned

for the city we call home: *Hoz'doh.*
      The Hot Place. The word tugs us

out of the Appalachians, the landscape of my childhood,
      and sends us back, which is to say

westward, but first: down into the valley where I was made,
      where our language was used to abstract

all processes of production; next: into the letters
      M E D, and quick, before we're lost in a maze of fog and factory:

up and out again, westward, as promised.
      We're over the rolling hills and Tennessee swamplands,

over the Mississippi, which had long been
      a border in the mind past which all was unknown

and therefore clearer, over the river and through the Midlands,
      where Laura Fermi once felt, though perhaps in Italian,

the *impact of emptiness,* and before we feel
      it too keenly ourselves, I'm leaning toward the lavenders

and scarlets of Ruth's southwestern sky. But not to be too-long distracted,
  not to linger, not to be so moved by the New Mexico piñon,

not to be entranced like the scientist's wife by the rocks
  that appeared as *cathedrals of yore,*

To escape from Los Alamos, to have learned
  from the trap we've already set against ourselves,

have fallen into before—not to loiter again under
  that awning of history's wide-mouthed myths,

not to be ensnared, not to awe, not to be taken too-long back by
  what must have been the beauty of the bomb:

To pick at such light like the skittish kitten
  who just now visited the steps of this very porch,

who is now disappearing into the green,
  licking flakes of fast-seized tuna from her lips;

To run away, with what bits of shine and char we find,
  into the forest of the present.

III. ATOMS IN SURPRISING LIGHT

"Could a person mourn and be joyful simultaneously?"
—Pam Houston, *Deep Creek: Finding Hope in High Country*

SONG FOR A HOMETOWN PROPHET, YEARS AFTER MOVING AWAY

And what John saw—after he laid his face
to the ground, as he'd been asked
by the voice that had come to him—

what he saw was invasive,
like the charred smell rising through B.'s home
in the Phoenix predawn blue:

Seeing how the war would come
must have intruded on John's senses,
as smoke against the usual desert clear

now intrudes on mine, has triggered me
awake this morning. What John saw as he slept
must have triggered him: I can see

how, after his forty days of dreaming,
he must have stood abruptly,
dripping with the Appalachian dirt.

What was coursing through John when he woke
was as real as the color of his daughter's skin,
blue when diphtheria killed her.

And that he could see the coming factory,
where they would do the work to make
the earth shake—that he could see was as natural

as smelling a brushfire. Burnt oleander
is natural oleander, after all, though it smells
weirdly sweet, turned neon as it entered my dream;

this flare is my periphery, now, as I lie awake.
It's made all reds go pink: beside our bed,
a plastic glass now loud with color;

the Navajo blanket as if pulsing at my feet—
and threaded in it, clear as the purpose
that built the city where I was born,

the thought of B's sister, how her eyes
were bright from crying as she spoke
of the mines on the Navajo Nation,

about some five-hundred
contaminated buildings there;
how their mother played as a child in that dust:

how, against such glare, the black outlines
of our selves glow harder—
how what was coursing through John

when he woke must have felt
like an even hotter
burning on his tongue.

Each day of forty, a cluster of
uranium burst from the buds,
as if he'd licked the same Arizona dust:

For as John slept—as I see—it was a rebound
of the element, feeding back and shimmying up
through the Tennessee ridge,

coursing through the place where
they'd bring what was mined.
That's what touched his lips.

And on his eyelids, shut against the ground,
it was the soft shine from a bomb
that years away had already fallen.

What John saw when he woke,
through his white-wire hair, what he saw
was imprinted with this shine—

it fixed his vision,
                              as if into a magic-eye,
so that his loneliness first pixelated

then popped together. Quick,
the way only loneliness—
or fear of it—can.

MARICOPA COUNTY BLUES

I sought you out, he'd told me—
    looked for me insistently,
looked the way our county now looks
    for a lost girl, their search now ten-days

long. Their search with *renewed focus.* I can see them
    circling places of *known visitation* in red,
hear the felt marker squeak
    with what's left of their hope.

Insistent, too: This new press of him
    against me. How egret feathers push out finer
and whiter down the breast
    and the back. How I want

that girl to be found, for her story
    to be more livable
than one imagines here, alone near
    where she disappeared.

And even though her loss
    must mean little to me if you were to turn
to those who lost her,
    it somehow swells inside me, grows so that

I think of her with
    each glow moving in the chunks of peripheral sky.
These planes glide toward me tonight
    like carolers who'd have me open up,

    swallow their fistfuls of light—
    tonight, the first night I've been sure
I could miss him, so soon
    it bowls me over, so soon

the grief I've thieved becomes
    my protector.

MOON BOX

1.
The cell knows how to divide itself,
no chemist's touch, no sterile glove,
just the single cell knitting more
cells from itself,
like a creepy neighbor
in that front room
wanting a lamp.
I walk away from her sepia slate
and long-fingered blinds
by taste-testing some metaphor
leftovers. I try *organ sacks* and
intestine snakes, both so silly
I might not think about the way
my gut shakes everything I need
into shit cocktails,
of that espresso martini I drank—
luscious froth of caffeine and vodka swirling
like pure light down the gullet gorge,
right around when BDF was having its own
circular party inside another particular room.

2.
By BDF I mean *Bilaminar Disc Formation,*
but it sounds like something the college kids
next door would say, doesn't it?
See you at the BDF, a rave
that would have benefited
from a couple of glow sticks at least,
but no, that room's dark, too,
and just the thought of human appendages
bouncing around in there is enough to send
me frantic after more words,
words that go like a faulty lathe,
trying to shape what's underneath
my tightening skin—
words that won't help me

process this for a father or a friend,
not even for you, even if
you're the kind of person who would
send my alloys into space, just for the thrill of it,
like the moon boxes Y-12 commissioned.

3.

Exceptionally well-made boxes,
them, used to carry out vials of blood
and bring them back with *structural*
and vacuum integrity; what we learned
from them was that nothing
inside them had changed. Space is a go.

4.
My step-father composed some
bits for these sound boxes.
Lost half a finger
in the same machine.
We're different beasts,
me and him, but I understand why his ego
glows, here—I get why we go up
and away, why my head tilts
at the fighter jet
scorching the sky
in all its abstraction.
I roll on an axis toward the fiction there.

SECRET CITY FESTIVAL

You cannot bank away.
Even as a plane pivots,
it empties your belly

only to fill it up again;
you're nauseous with the mix
of here and there,

a bodily impression of rising
even as you sink.
You cannot bank away,

must return, every
season, to the town
where you were born.

After four years in a desert,
you miss the reliability
of change: How,

in August, when a lawnmower's
undulations die down
and the bearer returns,

he will be covered in sweat,
clammy and irritable,
like a raincloud

wrapped in cheesecloth;
and still, one month later,
the leaves will blaze

their blood-orange drama
of descent. Unremarkable,
until it isn't.

When cold gives way to colder,
you're back again
for the grayness overhead,

for fog relentless over the Clinch.
Or else you phone your mother,
press her: *Can you hear the valley*

whipped with wind,
the crack of it
in your upper ear?

But even the Maypole
braids its billowed tulip-colors
around some unnamable shame

within you, spiked sharp at the end—
like the steel they've staked,
for the festival, into the crumbling

shale of Black Oak Ridge.
To dance around,
as if it were a glory.

ELIZABETH BISHOP VISITS ATOM CITY

She isn't fabled to have been here—a town
raised from valley mud in the scurry of a war

she spent in Florida. But say she'd driven north
alone, through the panhandle, where she'd

have seen the oil-rigs bloom and thought of
bosques, or skillets, maybe—the rusty brown

they turn unused, the pleasanter brown
of bacon grease, popping like a sharp maternal tsk.

Let's say she's driving now through Georgia,
up some Appalachian switchbacks:

Does she experience whiplash? Does the South
pull her with the hiccup motion of a heart,

and Uranium, in its abstraction, glare like a beacon
up ahead? And when she finds the cement gates

that flank a washed-out gravel road, I wonder
if she wonders at such lack of color, there,

amidst all that yellowing green—if she writes
Elza Gate and tries to smell hibiscus,

recalls a book of stately illustrations.
I'd wager when she isn't ushered in

like those with badges, she stops to see
a tulip poplar's whirring seeds, and, tucked

between the slapdash rafters, a hornet's nest,
doused and stilled, like exquisite pottery.

SCENE WITH GRANNY AND APPLE TREE

Kingsport 2011

Nor, for that matter, am I glad. Thankful,
yes. I can wake and fix me something to eat.

May is like this—small but measurable
necessities rise up from the apples beached

on the lawn: what I mean is, the grass pokes
like chin hairs through them. After so long a lay—

one wouldn't have tasted them—any globes
would go soft. Like a fleshy sea beneath the toupee

of spring. My body's bigger than the one I still chauffeur
in dreams. At Christmastime, dressed and perfumed

in department store goods, I'll watch a Kroger
ham with my greens devoured. So groomed

I'll be as the kids open their treats. So dutifully
they line up to hug the thing of me.

WAYS IN WHICH OTHERS DRESSING ME HAVE PROVED I'M LOVED

—The most obvious being
the gentle zip
toward the back of my neck,
his breath heavy as water.
—Before our wedding,
his mother slipping
the rug dress over my head,
down and over the same
spot of neck, hovering beside me
in the stiffness of the weave for longer
than you might expect, unembarrassed
by the gaudy light effect
of my bra, fuchsia
and pulsing by her bangs.
—Her fingers
working like a cellist's
at my waist as she tucks
the first belt to prepare for
the next, with which
her blue flowers
will further adorn me.
How his father
rushes to hold
the cinch around which
the belts belong,
the three of us wobbling,
like a bouquet of balloons
carried up stairs. —At the landing,
the painting in which my own mother
has dressed me twice:
first with the slow roll
of white tights
and the slip, toe-to-heel,
into tiny leather flats;
then in layers of oil, each
recreating more precisely
our small moment together—

How she shaded and re-shaded
the contours
of my body
and the negative space around it,
the space she knows best,
for it's always that I'm leaving
her. —And yesterday,
rummaging through the outfits Granny
left me, when I chose
one to wear without even washing
it first, and of course it's her hands
at every button, no longer
swollen, but nimble,
tracing the seams
of the dress that fit her
at thirty, climbing
upward until they reach
the collar at—again, my neck,
where all of this
could have gone wrong
but didn't.

CLEANING OUT THE KINGSPORT HOUSE

Each second, the earth is struck hard
by four and a half pounds of sunlight,

which means the weight of five pocketbooks,
immaculately kept, the small comb
zipped in a side pocket, too;

or else it means the pouring down on us
of a hair-dryer in its '92 Con-Air box—
two pounds plus a cord wound round

the wired tail of Porcelain Jesus,
who glows red when you spin
his wheel-click switch.

Each second on us
the weight of these items left
in the back corner of the back room

of my grandmother's house.
In the living room, the blinds
shut and the radio on,

my cousin apologizes for being sad
the way southern women usually do.

IF I INHABIT THESE I INHABIT DAD

diagonal inlay, lacing his mahogany desk like the idea of chess

envelop of stapled plastic, where I might keep a silver Bust Half company

the larger collection a stranger keeps, each coin minted in the year her father was born

1953

a letter I wrote in ninety-four, kept these twenty-five years & proof I've always been obsessed with time

... *your today, which is my tomorrow. Confusing, isn't it?!*

the house in the dream which is wrong but close enough, sliding off a Kingsport bluff, but close enough

glory of water unbridled from the bathroom faucet, but this is just another memory, isn't it,

and all the little shot-glass soldiers are moving in ways I can't foresee

       toward a party he never had, because a shot-glass chessboard is ridiculous, isn't it,

and, Did I give this to him?

What were my other meager gifts?

all of YouTube, for its dj potential, but most eerily

Celestial White Noise, subtitled

OOOOOOOOOOOOOOOOOOOOOOOOOOOOOOOOOOOOOOOOOOOOOOOOOOOOOOOOOOOOOOOOOOOOOOOO

IN THE VAST ARCHIVE OF ATOMS

We are told first and foremost that the archive is hot.
        I prefer to imagine the sun collecting itself   as if it were material
        first within my car   and then within
            my father's car, which is contained by mine   like a nesting doll
            and is hotter still at the very center.

Moving to the exterior of this figure, my forefinger blisters,
          absorbs a fleck of blue paint. The foreign body
             lodges there like a secret to return to, knowing I can't otherwise touch
                the ongoing largess of the archive, an   expanse that
                resembles my grief
                        precisely because it could never encompass it—
                          what Borges describes as spherical.
Circumference unknown.
   And what else do we know about everything we do not?
   I can tell you it upsets the skin.
        I want to understand, but I am always alone,
        always limited by my faculties. Let me return
                      to the greenhouse figure of my car,
inside which heat still multiplies.
   I cannot see beyond the glare of my making:
        We have been told, in so many words, that seeing inside the archive is
        metaphysical, but I am simple.
            I want to think of see *as touch.*
            As an experiment, I enter my description

of the archive, go again and again over
the endless boredom of factory leather,
        its many tiny punctures.
        I lay a palm on the ongoing dots,
            hoping they will speak to larger constellations,
            make sly remarks on what's been removed.

was not expecting
        to find snow here.
        I am almost certain it is ash.
            I can't see what has curled so into itself

that it has become something else: The light inside my image is so dull after all, and the smell so vague and sour.

Easily traded for a memory I might more readily

describe. What else am I left to work with, beyond the remainder of a trip
we once took, sludge inside the symbol of a coffee mug, circling underfoot?
Because I can't hold onto pure hypothesis,
I listen. You learn more about me when I say how doggedly I lean in, even
here, where there's no structure for emotion.
The soundtrack is inaudible
and unsung. Each song obscures
the face of the singer.

In the car I hear
my father's body strummed over again in its unraveling;

and so astounded by its loveliness am I,
I cannot help but press repeat.

DECAYED GHAZAL

The law of conservation of parity was wrong, Chien-Shiung
proved so. The men she proved so for won the nobel prize for Chien-Shiung.

A novelty calendar teaches me her name; she helped us fuel the bomb and
                                            understand decay.
Inherently likeable in its cobalt furs, Chien-Shiung's beta decay

says *scintillator* and yet stays far away from issues of consent.
Conservation of parity trusted nature to be symmetrical, in agreement

with itself; how like a mime you raise your glass and I raise mine,
how in the mirror I'm berating myself berating myself, uniformly,

only we're zoomed way in, now, and I never took physics. I always wanted
my head spun round in other ways. But now I want

to know: Is there a problem to chew on so tasty
I might, to my very last, doubt? I want to see my mouth

still puckering, *cosmological constant* a candy in my mouth
before two chalkboard balls that bob the thought of particles.

Don't they look like surly clowns? I think they would laugh,
if they could, at their jumbo size, their chalky solidity,

at my funny little need to know, and me,
plumbing me, still, up until the very last.

IN LIEU OF *ELEISON*, GIVE ME

back my step-brother's
name   in lieu of
hooking up with
the performative tenor

put his supple song
in my throat   in lieu of
my friend's flaked lips
please,   morning,

press your boring pleasures
on him   in lieu of *kyrie*
in lieu of the dream
in which I drink myself

further into dream
and lose my husband's face,
let me shave a bone nib
of my love for him

from my manubrium core,
let me chart how my loneliness
folds   for I know I will
bring myself

here again   in lieu of a daughter
who spades for
bulbs exactly rounded
let me lay my cheek

against softer memories
of my mother's voice
each time
    she speaks

instead of directions, Dad—
left on Linden—
let me go back
        let me go back

let me describe to you
the mood of your
wellbeing I prayed for
the woodland creatures there

NOTES

The title "But Think, Are You Authorized to Tell It" was borrowed from wartime propaganda urging secrecy.

The poems "Manufacturing" through "Targeting" are named after a building in an early spatial concept for the Manhattan Project site at Oak Ridge (*Atomic Spaces*, Peter Bacon Hales).

Language and anecdotes from the life of John Hendrix are woven throughout the collection. He was a rural community member in Oak Ridge Valley before the Manhattan Project came to the area; he also supposedly foresaw the atom bomb in the 1910s, after the death of his daughter, the abandonment by his wife, and the experience of a religious conversion.

Granny's voice is written in memory of my own, who was born and raised in rural western Virginia.

"What You See Here" takes its title from Oak Ridge's "Guardian Monkey" billboard.

"Perhaps *lucky* is too casual" is a quotation from Richard Falk's article in *Guernica*, "The Weird 'Good Fortune' of Tsutomu Yamaguchi."

"Think of Sleep" is after April Naoko Heck's "I Don't Have Hands That Caress My Face."

"Elizabeth Bishop Visits Atom City" is after Jake Adam York's "Walt Whitman in Alabama."

"Cleaning Out the Kingsport House" gets its physics and first two lines from a Charles Wright poem, "In Praise of Thomas Hardy."

cknowledgements

Michael Frayn's play, *Copenhagen*, Heisenberg illustrates his conception of
e Uncertainty Principle: "Walking round Faelled Park on my own one horrible
w February night. It's very late, and as soon as I've turned off into the park I'm
mpletely alone in the darkness. I start to think about what you'd see, if you could
in a telescope on me from the mountains of Norway. You'd see me by the street
nps on the Blegdamsvej, then nothing as I vanished into the darkness, then
other glimpse of me as I passed the lamp-post in front of the bandstand. And
at's what we see in the cloud chamber. Not a continuous track but a series of
mpses - a series of collisions between the passing electron and various atoms of
ter vapour...."

ike to imagine what you would see, if you'd trained a telescope on me as I was
iting this book. In between the long stretches of uncertainty, you'd catch glimpses
me, chewing on a straw, trying to get the idea out. You'd also see who I was
rtunate enough to collide with along the way:

rst, my teachers. Thank you to the eighth grade teacher who showed me poems
Langston Hughes and Gwendolyn Brooks, establishing from the beginning of
y poetic education that verse was not separate from life and history, but a vital
rt of it; to Jane Sasser, who permitted me to try and figure out what a literary
agazine was on an old Compaq computer at ORHS. To Alan Michael Parker,
10 believed me when I said I wanted to be a poet and has continued to help me
come one, long after I left campus, and to Suzanne Churchill: Thank you, thank
u, for your Modern American Poetry class. Thanks to Cynthia Hogue, Sally Ball,
d Norman Dubie, who have challenged me, each with their own genius, to write
e poems I really needed to write.

ext, thanks to the friends who helped me do so: Rachel Andoga, Michele Poulos,
ark Haunschild, David Moody, Katie Berta, Sarah Miller, Jess Smith, Sarah Hynes,
att Bell, and so many more talented writers who have graciously taught me some
what they know. Thanks to the word-loving folks in Phoenix, who made even 115
gree weather tolerable, and to those in Tucson, who have so heartily welcomed
e. Thank you to Kristin Apple, whose monotype print spoke to some unable part
me, and to all of our Davidson friends; I am always trying to be worthy of their
llective warmth and intelligence. Thanks to Mary Robbins, Elena DiRosa, Becca
ller and Kelly Gannon—the badass women who got me through my years in
anada and New York City. To all of the Ridgers, who embrace my quirks when

I return home, but in particular: Kendahl Moore and Joel Hewett, who condu
archival research on Oak Ridge for fun.

To my mother and Larry; to my family, in both Tennessee and Arizona—I love y
all; you have always encouraged my curiosity, and I am in your debt.

Lastly, to Bojan, who, to my endless good fortune, is my partner in both poet
and in life: This book would certainly not have existed without your unflinchi
support.

Sara Sams is a writer from Oak Ridge, Tennessee, a lab town developed in secret to enrich uranium during World War II. She is currently researching the influence particle physics has had on contemporary poetics and learning how to be a mom. Sara has spent much of the past decade in Arizona and teaches writing at the University of Arizona. Between 2013 and 2016, she received fellowships to teach at the National University of Singapore and for the Ministry of Education in Logroño, Spain. A graduate of Davidson College and Arizona State University (M.F.A.), her poems and translations have appeared in *Blackbird, The Volta, Matter Monthly, The Drunken Boat, Now & Then: The Appalachian Magazine*, and elsewhere. You can find her work online at saraesams.com.

Printed in the USA
CPSIA information can be obtained
at www.ICGtesting.com
LVHW071233190923
758462LV00007B/396

9 781646 624966